A Glacier
Viewed From
An Ice
Cave In
The Alps

FACES
AND
PLACES

SWITZERLAND

BY PAMELA K. HARRIS
AND BRAD CLEMMONS

THE CHILD'S WORLD®, INC.

COVER PHOTO

A boy wearing traditional clothing in Murren.
©Ric Ergenbright/CORBIS

Published in the United States of America by The Child's World®, Inc.
PO Box 326
Chanhassen, MN 55317-0326
800-599-READ
www.childsworld.com

Project Manager James R. Rothaus/James R. Rothaus & Associates
Designer Robert E. Bonaker/R. E. Bonaker & Associates
Contributors Mary Berendes, Dawn M. Dionne, Katherine Stevenson, Ph.D., Red Line Editorial

Library of Congress Cataloging-in-Publication Data
Harris, Pamela K., 1962-
Switzerland / by Pamela K. Harris and Brad Clemmons.
p. cm.
Includes index.
ISBN 1-56766-912-3 (alk. paper)
1. Switzerland—Juvenile Literature.
[1. Switzerland]
I. Clemmons, Brad. II. Title.
DQ17 .H35 2001
949.4—dc21

Table of Contents

If you could see Earth from outer space, you would see large areas of land called **continents**. One land area is the largest of all. Its eastern part is called Asia, and its western part is called Europe. Switzerland is in Europe.

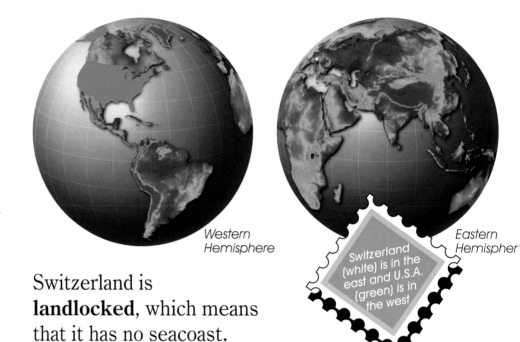

Western Hemisphere

Eastern Hemispher

Switzerland (white) is in the east and U.S.A. (green) is in the west

Switzerland is **landlocked**, which means that it has no seacoast. It is surrounded by five other countries.

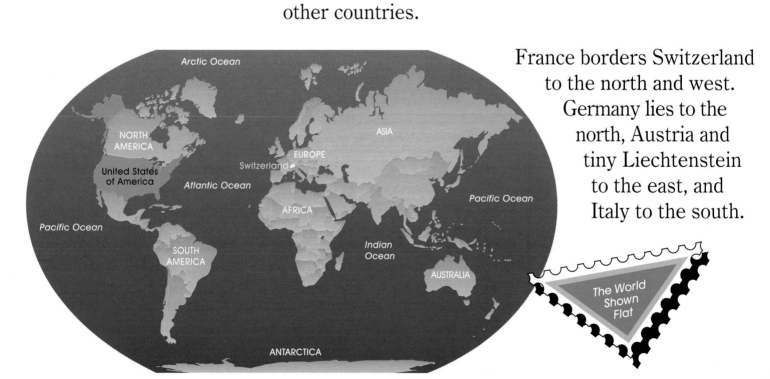

France borders Switzerland to the north and west. Germany lies to the north, Austria and tiny Liechtenstein to the east, and Italy to the south.

The World Shown Flat

6

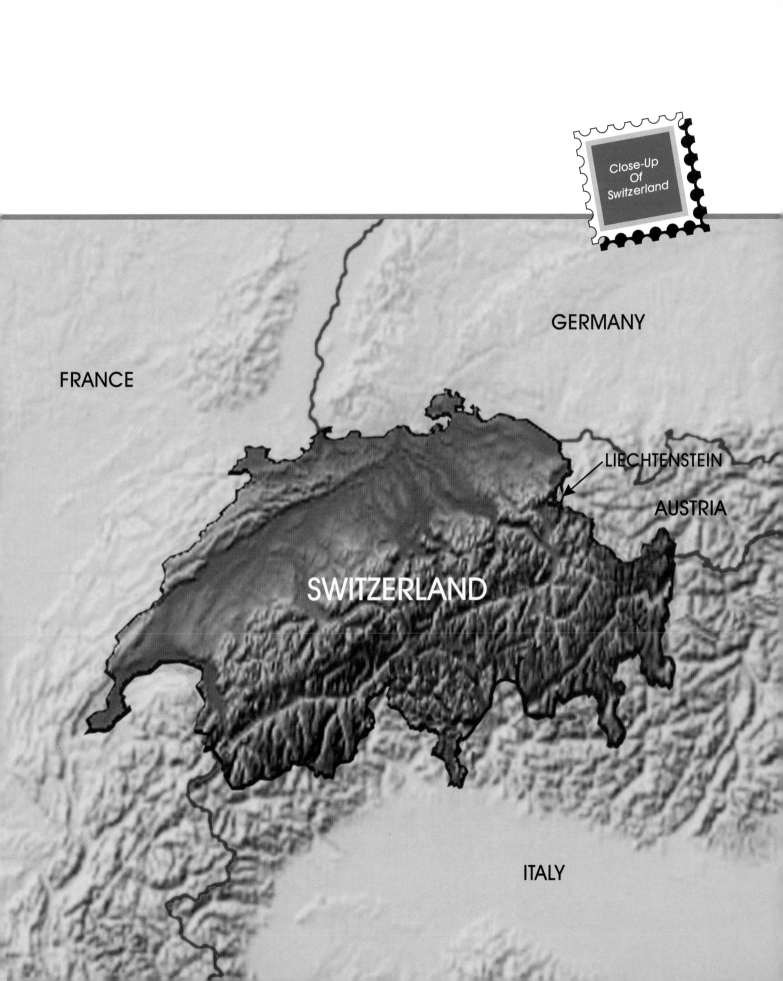

FRANCE

GERMANY

LIECHTENSTEIN

AUSTRIA

SWITZERLAND

ITALY

Close-Up
Of
Switzerland

Rhein Falls
Near
Schaffhausen

Schaffhausen

JURA MOUNTAINS

MITTELLAND

A L P S

Lauterbrunnen

Matterhorn ▲ Dufourspitze

©Bob Krist/CORBIS

Farms In Lauterbrunnen

©Craig Aurness/CORBIS

Switzerland is very mountainous, especially around its borders. The Jura (YOO-rah) Mountains are in the north and west, and the Alps are in the south and east. The Matterhorn, Switzerland's most famous mountain, is in the Alps. Switzerland's highest peak is *Dufourspitze* (doo-FOR-shpit-zeh), which stands 15,203 feet tall.

The Matterhorn

©Ralph Starkweather/CORBIS

Central Switzerland is called the *Mittelland,* German for "middle land." This scenic area has rolling hills and views of spectacular mountains in the distance. It also has deep valleys with streams and beautiful waterfalls. The weather in the central region is milder than in the snow-capped mountains.

Switzerland's plant life varies with the height of the land. Walnut, apple, pear, almond, and cherry trees grow on lower land. Higher in the mountains, pine and fir trees are more common. Above 10,000 feet, alpine meadows are filled with edelweiss, alpenroses, and other wildflowers. Some wildflowers bloom for only one week every year.

An Alpine Ibex In The Valais Region

A Shepherd's Fritallary Butterfly

©O. Alamany & E. Vicens/CORBIS

The Alps are home to most of Switzerland's wildlife, including foxes, deer, and small antelopes called chamois (SHAM-ee). The ibex, a mountain goat, was brought back to the Alps after it became **extinct** in the area. Birds are common throughout the land. Fish such as salmon and trout swim in the streams and rivers. Many animals live in the Swiss National Park, a 70-square-mile wildlife preserve in southeast Switzerland.

©Frank Lane Picture Agency/CORBIS

ALPS

VALAIS

Swiss
National
Park

Snow-covered
Alpine Trees

©Paul Almassy/CORBIS

Soldiers
Taking A Break
In Bern During
Napoleon's
Time

★ Bern

• Bellinzona

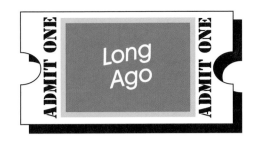

Long Ago

More than 30,000 years ago, most of Switzerland was covered with a thick sheet of ice that flowed down from the mountains. As the land warmed up, people began to settle in Switzerland. They learned to farm and fish in the river valleys. By 850 B.C., central Switzerland was controlled by the Helvetii, a powerful tribe of **Celts** (KELTS). Julius Caesar and the Romans conquered the Helvetii in 58 B.C. Almost 600 years later, the Romans fell to Germanic tribes that included the Alemanni and the Franks.

Charlemagne was emperor of the **Holy Roman Empire** in the late 700s and early 800s. He ruled most of Europe, including Switzerland. In 1798, Napoleon invaded Switzerland and created the Helvetic Republic.

After Napoleon's defeat in 1815, the country was left without a constitution. The Swiss Federal Constitution, modeled after the Constitution of the United States, was created in 1848. It balanced power and decision making between the federal and local governments.

Montebello Castle in Bellinzona

Today Switzerland is a prosperous country that plays a major role in international banking and business. The nation's laws are made by a **parliament** of elected representatives and a council of seven key leaders. The country is divided into areas called *cantons,* which are like the states of the United States. Each canton has its own local government.

For hundreds of years the Swiss have practiced **neutrality**—refusing to take sides when other nations disagree. They maintained their neutrality during the First and Second World Wars. More recently, they have declined to join the European Union, a group of 15 European countries that work together.

Switzerland's neutrality has made it a center for some international organizations, such as the United Nations and the International Red Cross.

The City Hall Building In Lucerne

Lucerne

★ Bern

©Wolfgang Kaehler/CORBIS

Bundeshaus,
The Swiss
Houses Of
Parliament
In Bern

A Couple
At A Sidewalk
Cafe In
Zürich

• Zürich

Lake Geneva

A Woman Organ Grinder

©Keren Su/CORBIS

Switzerland has one of the most mixed populations in Europe. The people, customs, and languages are a mixture of German, French, and Italian influences from neighboring lands. One-fifth of the people are **immigrants** who have come from other parts of Europe. Switzerland also has immigrants from other areas of the world, including Africa, India, and Southeast Asia.

A Fisherman Holding His Catch At Lake Geneva

©Nathan Benn/CORBIS

Most of Switzerland's people are Christians, either Roman Catholic or Protestant. The Protestant religion was formed centuries ago when a group of people split from the Catholic Church. The split led to some of Switzerland's worst fighting. Other religions practiced in Switzerland today include the Jewish, Islamic, and Greek Orthodox faiths.

Children Pulling A Milk Cart In Emdthal

©Sandro Vannini/CORBIS

Most of Switzerland's people live in cities or smaller towns. Zürich is the largest city, with almost one million residents. Bern is the capital of Switzerland. In the cities, most people work in office buildings, shops, or banks. In the summer, they meet for coffee in outdoor cafes. Many people ride streetcars to work instead of driving cars.

A Streetcar Running Through A Town

Although most of Switzerland is mountainous, relatively few people live in the mountains. In these alpine regions, farmers raise dairy cows that produce milk and cheese. Other farmers tend **vineyards** that grow grapes for making wine. Some farmers grow fruits for preserves and desserts. Country farmhouses are often decorated with giant cowbells.

©Milepost 92°/CORBIS

©Paul Almasy/CORBIS

• Zürich

★ Bern

• Emdthal

A
Classroom
In
Trogen

Trogen •

S

• Brienz

A L P

• Geneva

Children begin primary school at age six or seven and continue through grade nine. After that, they have two choices. They can either go to high school or take a *lehre* (LAY-reh). A lehre is an apprenticeship for learning a trade such as carpentry or plumbing.

Switzerland has four languages: German, French, Italian, and Romansch. Two-thirds of the people speak a **dialect**, or type, of German called *Schwyzertütsch.* (SHVY-tser-tootsh) People in Geneva and the west speak French. Italian is spoken in southern Switzerland.

A Sign Asks Motorists To Turn Off Their Car Engines At A Red Light

An Apprentice Woodcarver At A School In Brienz

A few people in the eastern Alps speak Romansch, a very old language. Many Swiss people know two, three, or even four languages. Sometimes when two people talk, each person is speaking a different language!

Work

A Farmer Carrying His Tools

More than half of Switzerland's people work in jobs that provide some kind of service for other people. Switzerland is an international banking center, and many people work in banking-related jobs. Providing services for **tourists**, or visitors, is another important business.

Switzerland has fairly poor soil, and few people make their living from farming. Many more work in manufacturing. Switzerland has few natural resources of its own. Instead, the Swiss must buy raw materials from other countries and then sell back the manufactured goods.

Swiss factories make machinery, chemicals, clothing, and food. Swiss-made clocks and watches are especially famous.

An Aircraft Mechanic Working On A Jet Engine In Zürich

Zürich

Geneva

A Worker In A Control Room At A Nuclear Research Facility In Geneva

A Sidewalk
Cafe In
Lausanne

• Burgenstock

Lausanne •

VALAIS

©Morton Beebe, S.F./CORBIS

Kronenbourg LE RAISIN Kronenbourg

HOTEL & CAFE DU RAISIN

Kronenbourg   Kronenbourg   Kronenbourg

Swiss foods show influences from German, French, and Italian cooking styles. Different regions of the country have different specialties. Among Switzerland's most famous foods are fine chocolate, wines, and *muesli* (MYOO-slee), a kind of whole-grain breakfast cereal.

Chefs At A Table Of Food In Burgenstock

©Bob Krist/CORBIS

Switzerland is also known for its cheeses. The best-known kind, Swiss cheese, is famous for its holes!

Slicing Cheese At A Restaurant In Valais

©Sandro Vannini/CORBIS

Gruyère and Emmentaler cheeses are melted together to make a famous Swiss dish called *fondue* (fon-DOO). To eat fondue, people put pieces of bread on long-handled forks and dip them into the melted cheese. *Raclette* (rah-KLET) is another favorite dish. It is simply melted cheese that is served over potatoes.

Pastimes And Holidays

ADMIT ONE · ADMIT ONE

People travel from all over the world to ski in the Swiss mountains. Downhill and cross-country skiing are both popular. Swiss people enjoy many other outdoor sports, too, such as hiking, mountain climbing, and cycling.

Swiss people celebrate a number of holidays, including New Year's Day, Easter, and Christmas. On Swiss National Day (August 1), people celebrate the nation's origins with mountaintop bonfires and city fireworks.

Basler Fasnacht is a three-day festival during Lent that begins with a parade—at 4 o'clock in the morning! The parade features clubs, or *cliques* (KLIKS), of costumed members playing drums and piccolos and carrying candle-lit lanterns.

Switzerland is a country of many contrasts. High jagged mountain peaks and flat green valleys make up the landscape. Swiss culture blends languages and customs from other countries with its own unique folk traditions. Today, many important leaders come to Switzerland to discuss health, economic, and political issues. Though Switzerland is a small country, it has an important role in world history.

A Mountaineer On A Peak Near The Valais Region

©Roger Antrobus/CORBIS

26

Basel • • Rhine River

• Zürich

★ Bern

Lausanne •

Geneva •

Rhône River

Rhine River

VALAIS

Lake Lugano

©Charles & Jesette Lenars/CORBIS

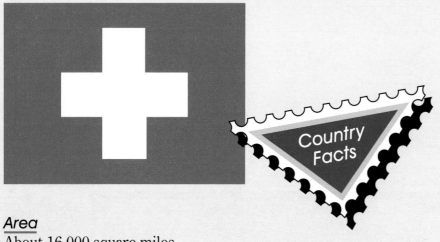

Area
About 16,000 square miles
(41,000 square kilometers)—about twice as big as Massachusetts.

Population
Over 7 million people.

Capital City
Bern.

Other Important Cities
Zürich, Geneva, Basel, and Lausanne.

Important Rivers
The Rhine and the Rhône.

Money
The Swiss franc (FRANHK), which is divided into 100 centimes (SAHN-teem), called *rappen* (RAHP-pen) in the German regions.

National Flag
A white cross on a red background. The cross originally stood for the Christian religion, but now it also represents Switzerland's neutrality. The flag of the International Red Cross is modeled after the Swiss flag.

National Song
"Swiss Anthem."

Heads of Government
The president and the Bundesrat of Switzerland. The Bundesrat is a federal council made up of 7 members.

Official Name
The Swiss Confederation (*Schweizerische Eidgenossenschaft* in German, *Coféderation Suisse* in French, *Connfederazione Svizzera* in Italian, and *Confederaziun Helvetica* in Romansch).

A Man
Playing An
Alpenhorn

Switzerland
Trivia

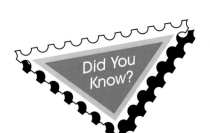

Did You
Know?

Switzerland has been home to many scholars, scientists, and inventors. Swiss people invented products ranging from cellophane to dried soup to milk chocolate! One Swiss man noticed the burrs that stuck to his dog when they went for walks in the mountains. He copied the way the burrs worked and invented the Velcro® fastener!

The World Wide Web was invented by a scientist working at the CERN research institute near Geneva.

The famous children's book Heidi was written by a woman named Johanna Spyri, who grew up near Zürich. She wrote the story for her son and based it on her own childhood.

In the Alps along the Italian border, Saint Bernard dogs are trained to track and rescue hikers lost in the mountains.

Lake Lugano in southern Switzerland has an island covered with tropical plants such as palm trees.

How
Do You
Say?

	GERMAN	HOW TO SAY IT
Hello	guten tag	GOO–ten TAHK
Good-bye	auf wiedersehen	owf VEE–der–zeyn
Thank You	danke	DAHN–keh
	SWISS GERMAN	HOW TO SAY IT
Hello	gruezi	GROO–e–zee
Good-bye	uf widerluege	uf VEE–der–loo–guh
Thank You	merci villmool	mehr–SEE VEEL–mool
	FRENCH	HOW TO SAY IT
Hello	bonjour	bohn–ZHOOR
Good-bye	au revoir	oh reh–VWAHR
Thank You	merci	mehr–SEE
	ITALIAN	HOW TO SAY IT
Hello	buon giorno	bwon JYOR–noh
Good-bye	arrivederci	a–ree–va–DARE–chay
Thank You	grazie	GRAH–zee–ay
	ROMANSCH	HOW TO SAY IT
Hello	buna sera	BOON–uh SAIR–uh
Good-bye	tchau	CHOW
Please	per plaschair	pair PLAY–jair

Celts (KELTS)
The Celts were a group of people who lived in Europe thousands of years ago. Central Switzerland was once controlled by a tribe of Celts called the Helvetii.

continents (KON-tih-nents)
Earth's continents are huge land areas surrounded mostly by water. The largest continent has Europe on the western end and Asia on the eastern end.

dialect (DY-uh-lekt)
A dialect is a different form of a language that is spoken in a particular region or by a particular group. Many Swiss people speak a dialect of German.

extinct (ex-TINKT)
An extinct animal or plant is one that has died out altogether. Ibex became extinct in the Alps and had to be reintroduced.

Holy Roman Empire (HOH-lee ROH-man EM-pire)
The Holy Roman Empire existed between the years 800 and 1806. It was a group of countries and territories that were controlled by just one leader at a time, rather than by many. Charlemagne ruled the Empire in the late 700s.

immigrants (IM-mih-grents)
Immigrants are people who move to a land from somewhere else. Switzerland has immigrants from other nations in Europe and around the world.

landlocked (LAND-lokt)
A landlocked country is surrounded by land rather than being next to an ocean or sea. Switzerland is landlocked.

neutrality (noo-TRAL-ih-tee)
Being neutral is avoiding taking a side in a war or political conflict. Switzerland follows a policy of neutrality in international affairs.

parliament (PAR-leh-ment)
A parliament is a group of elected leaders that make a nation's laws. Switzerland has a parliament.

tourists (TOOR-ists)
Tourists are people who travel to a place to visit and sightsee. Many tourists visit Switzerland.

vineyards (VIN-yerdz)
Vineyards are farms where grapes are grown and made into wine. Switzerland has vineyards.

Index

Web Sites

Learn more about Switzerland:
http://www.switzerland.com
http://www.visiteurope.com/Switzerland/
http://www.lonelyplanet.com/destinations/europe/switzerland/

Read about current news, events, and culture in Switzerland:
http://www.swissinfo.org/eng

Hear examples of Switzerland's four languages:
http://www.schweiz-in-sicht.ch/en/uebersicht/uebersicht.html
(Click on "Federalism and Multilingualism" and then click on "The Four National Languages" on the side.)

Listen to Switzerland's national anthem:
http://www.lengua.com/hymnen.htm
(Click on "National Anthem of Switzerland.")